TEAM
BUILDING
in Church Groups

Nancy Geyer and Shirley Noll

JUDSON PRESS, Valley Forge

TEAM BUILDING IN CHURCH GROUPS

Copyright © 1970
Judson Press
Valley Forge, Pa. 19481

The Bible verses in this volume are in accordance with *The New English Bible, New Testament,* © The Delegates of the Oxford University Press and The Syndics of the Cambridge University Press 1961.

Standard Book No. 8170-0480-7
Library of Congress Catalog Card No. 76-107653

Printed in the U.S.A.

CONTENTS

1.
Introduction to Team Building

For Christ is like a single body with its many limbs and organs, which, many as they are, together make up one body. . . .

A body is not one single organ, but many. Suppose the foot should say, "Because I am not a hand, I do not belong to the body," it does belong to the body none the less. Suppose the ear were to say, "Because I am not an eye, I do not belong to the body," it does still belong to the body. If the body were all eye, how could it hear? If the body were all ear, how could it smell? But, in fact, God appointed each limb and organ to its own place in the body, as he chose. . . .

But God has combined the various parts of the body, giving special honour to the humbler parts, so that there might be no sense of division in the body, but that all its organs might feel the same concern for one another. If one organ suffers, they all suffer together. If one flourishes, they all rejoice together.

1 Corinthians 12:12, 14-18, 25-26, NEB

The dynamic process of team building is one way Christians may experience being "one body in Christ." In the church a team is any group of people who work together on a common task. They may be the Board of Christian Education, the teaching staff as a whole or as departments, persons working together with children or youth or adults, deacons, deaconesses, trustees, church boards, the leaders of women's or men's groups, or the staff of a special school of missions or other similar programs. Through their actions the task is completed; through their interactions a team is built. Team building occurs as team members experience the unique and indispensable part each plays in accomplishing the common task.

The group as a whole needs to make the decision to be involved in team building. As a part of that decision they will designate one member to serve as leader who will be responsible to help the members recognize and fulfill the tasks of the group. This person may be the stated chairman of the group or he may be chosen by the group for the specific task of leadership in the team-building experience.

The Apostle Paul says, "But God has combined the various parts of the body, giving special honour to the humbler parts, so that there might be no sense of division in the body. . . ." "No sense of division" occurs as *every* member of the team begins to feel that no one individual has *more* or *less responsibility* than any other individual for making plans, for reaching decisions, for initiating action, for "success" or "failure." While each member carries equally the responsibility for the smooth functioning of the team, each one brings to the team his own unique background of experience and his own special gifts and skills. The gospel calls for Christians to share equally the responsibility for the job to be done. As team members freely offer their experiences, gifts, and skills to the team, they not only accept an equal share of responsibility but also show forth "the same concern for one another."

Full individual participation in listening, speaking, and acting is called for in team building in order that all members may feel the same concern for one another. When the team is working together, no idea, question, or concern related to the task is inconsequential or irrelevant. Each is important and deserves a response simply because it is a real question or concern of a member of the team. The team member will speak up, ask a question, state an idea, or ask that a suggestion be clarified. Part of each member's responsibility is to say directly and openly what he thinks and feels in order to give the other members the opportunity to hear and respond. Others on the team will then expect to be heard and responded to similarly.

Mutual, open sharing helps the team to feel the same concern for one another. When speaking to the group, each member of the team speaks only for himself as he offers his ideas, questions, and feelings. He may say "you" or "they" or "we," but essentially and underneath he is saying "I." In a basic sense he speaks only for himself. *His* unique, vital contribution is what *he* speaks. For team building, it is better to say, "I think," "I feel," "I believe," "I'll try."

"If one organ suffers, they all suffer together. If one flourishes, they all rejoice together." *Suffer* and *rejoice* are words which express feeling. Only as individual team members contribute openly their feelings, both positive and negative, can effective team building take place. An important part of each member's sharing of himself is for him to indicate when he agrees or disagrees with the ideas of his fellow team members. Often it is not easy to disagree. Honest disagreement is a *vital and valid offering of oneself* which is essential for suffering and rejoicing together. Through this sharing process, a team truly becomes "one body in Christ," where persons may work together on a common task, experiencing no sense of division and feeling the same concern for one another.

A teaching-learning experience occurs for persons within any group as the group develops and works together. Through the dynamic process of team building, both group development and the teaching-learning experience are enhanced. For all groups in the church that share a common task, these team building activities have merit.

GOALS OF TEAM BUILDING

These objectives are the goals of team building:
1. To express openly feelings, ideas, and questions related to the task.
2. To listen and respond directly to the feelings and ideas of other members of the team.
3. To act and feel as individuals sharing equal responsibility with every other individual on the team.
4. To enable the team to fulfill its task more effectively.

The following questions are based upon these goals and are suggested for team members to consider individually or as a total group after a session together:

How do I feel about my unique value as a member of this team?

How do I feel about the unique value of each of the other members of this team?

Right now, what division (if any) do I feel in our team?

Right now, how do I feel about our team's progress in fulfilling its task?

A BASIC PROCEDURE FOR EFFECTIVE TEAM BUILDING

A three-step, basic procedure is suggested for use every time a team experiences one of the activities in team building. The purpose of the procedure is to enable the team to derive specific learnings from work they do together. A key to successful team building lies in the team members trying some procedure together, looking at what happens, and deciding together what to do the next time.

Step 1 *Do something together:* Try an activity suggested in this booklet, or do another piece of work.

For example: Divide a group of twelve persons into three subgroups to suggest ideas for a new program. The subgroups report their ideas to the total group on newsprint.

Step 2 Discuss as a team: *What happened?* In what specific ways was what we tried helpful? In what specific ways was what we tried not helpful?

For example: What happened when we worked in subgroups? When we returned to the total group? Some team members may find the procedure helpful because of the full participation and the many ideas produced quickly in small groups. For other team members, the procedure may not be helpful because of confusion caused by too many ideas and by lengthy reports from other subgroups.

Step 3 Discuss as a team: *What have we learned?* Do we

For example: The team may learn that to suggest quickly a variety of ideas for a new

8

want to do this again? If so, do we want to do it the same way? (Or, how shall we do it differently? If not, why not?)

program while working in subgroups is effective. The team may decide to do this again with a variation: A smaller group, having one person from each subgroup, will meet separately to prepare for presentation at the following team meeting a proposal based on the ideas from all three subgroups.

Guidelines for Effective Team Meetings

The purpose of guidelines for team meetings is to provide simple, specific steps for implementing team development at any meeting. The way team meetings are conducted creates the backdrop for building team morale.

Setting and Climate

Always sit in a circle so that everyone can see everyone else. Communication is greatly helped when everyone can see and be seen. If a team member arrives late, open the circle and insist that he become a part of it.

Encourage every person to say what he thinks and feels.

Be alert during the meeting for signals that indicate unspoken concerns, your own or others', such as glancing at the clock, yawning, tapping a foot or fingers. Recognizing such a signal, say to the group: "I think we aren't getting anywhere," "We have only fifteen more minutes," or "We have been on this topic for half an hour; what can we do to reach a decision and move on?"

Spending Time Together

Clock time can be an important ally in team building. Take time to discuss openly and fully when the group will meet and for how long. Make realistic decisions based on your life situations and the common task you have to do. Resolve to begin and end on time.

Face squarely the questions of absenteeism and tardiness. Discuss how the members feel about some coming late, leaving early, missing meetings.

Speak directly to each other in the team to reveal feelings concerning tardiness or absenteeism. When a member will be absent next time, or has missed the last meeting, or when one has to leave early, reasons for such actions should be shared briefly.

When the team meeting is late starting or stopping, talk openly about how members feel regarding such delays.

Before you adjourn, check on the time, place, purpose, and date of the next meeting.

Building an Agenda Together

Use newsprint at *every* meeting for making public notes for the team. The use of newsprint helps every member of the team to be "on board" at all times. It permits everyone to see what tasks face the group, what decisions have to be made, and what conclusions are being reached. It eliminates the necessity of individual note taking and permits full participation by all members of the team.

Begin the session by hanging several blank sheets of newsprint where they are clearly visible to the group.

Spend 5 minutes allowing members spontaneously to suggest items for the agenda, the work they want to do together in this session.

10

Record *all* suggestions at this time.

Let the group decide which items to consider first and which to consider after further planning or at the next meeting.

Before working on any item of the agenda, find out from the person who suggested it: (1) if the item requires a group decision or action, (2) if he is looking for opinions from the group but not a decision, or (3) if he wants to give or receive information about the item.

Carrying Out the Agenda

Let the newsprint help you carry out the agenda.

Use newsprint to record *all* decisions and action plans.

Beside the job listed to be done, write the name of the person who agrees to do the job and the completion date agreed upon.

Use newsprint to present ideas, plans, or schedules to the group.

Keep the newsprint used during the meeting, and from it prepare *brief* notes for each member of the team. These should be distributed promptly to all team members.

2.
The First
Team-Building Session

Facing differences is the key to team building in early meetings. Sharing and exploring openly the differences in experiences, ideas, and feelings which individuals bring to the group provide the necessary strength for team building to occur. There are a number of possible activities for the first team-building efforts. No group or team will necessarily use all of these following activities:

An Activity to Explore "What I Would Like to Be Called" (a 20–30 minute session)

Purpose: To encourage the direct, personal expression of feelings among team members.

At your first meeting, ask each person to make a name tag for himself, writing in large letters the name he would prefer to be called by the group. The name tags are pinned to shirts or blouses and worn throughout the session.

Members of the group then ask each other how they feel about using the names others have asked to be called. If one would feel more comfortable calling someone else by a name not on his name tag, he should say so and give his reasons.

Be careful not to discuss *in general* what forms of name to use for everyone on the team. Work with each other's *individual* feelings to reach your decisions. For example, if Mary, a teenager, has always called an older person "Mr. Jones" and if he asks to be called "Tom," then he and Mary can decide whether she should try calling him "Tom" or whether Tom will expect her to call him "Mr. Jones" while others call him "Tom." If a pastor or other professional is on the team, his position can be clarified through this activity.

12

In each instance, decide by mutual consent what you will do.

ACTIVITIES TO DEVELOP TEAM OBJECTIVES

To work together well as a team, a group needs clearly stated objectives. These objectives should be based on the ideas and feelings of the members of the team. Only objectives which are real for the individual members of the team will be "team objectives." What someone outside the team recommends becomes a team objective only when team members accept it for themselves.

Purpose of these activities: To facilitate team building while developing team objectives.

A. For teams with both old and new members (45 minutes)

Step 1 —Divide into pairs with both persons being *old* members or both being *new* members. Spend 15 minutes in pairs discussing: "I feel that the *most important* objectives for the team or group are. . . ." Each person is asked to write on a half sheet of newsprint the two or three most important objectives of the other person in the pair.

Step 2 —Post the newsprint from each pair, grouping them according to old members and new members.

Step 3 —The total team discusses for 30 minutes:

What are the differences between the objectives stated by old members and new members?

What are the reasons for these differences?

What objectives appear most often on the sheets?

Which objectives will be adopted for the group?

One member should make copies of these objectives for the other team members. Keep these objectives for future evaluation. Post your objectives on newsprint at each team meeting.

B. For teams whose members know each other and have worked together before (90 minutes)

Step 1 — Work in groups of three (persons *a, b, c*) for 45

minutes. Put in each group persons who know each other well. Allow 15 minutes for each person. First, persons *b* and *c* tell person *a* what *they* believe he feels are the most important objectives for the team. *A* listens until they have finished. *A* then tells *b* and *c* where they were on target, where they were off target. *A*'s two or three most important objectives are then written on newsprint. Repeat for *b* and *c,* allowing 15 minutes for each.

Step 2 — Allow 10 minutes for reports from each group of three. Briefly each person tells what the other two said to him and then shares his objectives.

Step 3 — The total team discusses for 15 minutes:

What objectives appear most often on the sheets?

Which objectives will be adopted for the group?

As suggested in A above, one team member should be asked to make copies of these objectives for each team member and to keep the objectives for future evaluation. Post objectives on newsprint at each team meeting.

An Activity for Team Members
With Specific Responsibilities

Purpose: To provide an opportunity for all group members to reach an agreement about the way in which persons with specific responsibilities will carry them out in the group.

Teams often have a designated leader or chairman. Church teams often have a clergyman or other professional church worker as one of their members. Lay persons like the church school superintendent may have designated responsibilities on the team. When any team member has a specific responsibility, try the following:

Step 1 — For 10 minutes have the member with the special job or responsibility leave the group and write on newsprint: "What I would like to do to carry out my job as (chairman, pastor, etc.) in the group

14

is. . . ." The rest of the team is divided into groups of 4 or 5 and asked to write on newsprint: "What we would like the (chairman, pastor, etc.) to do to carry out his job in this group is. . . ."

Step 2 — Post newsprint and help the total team discuss for 15 minutes:

What are the areas of agreement?

What are the differences in what we would like?

How shall we resolve these differences?

Step 3 — For 5 minutes ask the (chairman, pastor, etc.) to explain how he understands the agreement between the group and himself about the way he will carry out his job.

3.
Later Team-
Building Sessions

In the first two or three team meetings, team-building activities need to focus on basic guidelines for conducting effective meetings, such as using newsprint, building an agenda together, paying attention to clock time, and attendance. Also warranting attention in early meetings are activities which focus on personal concern for one another, such as those described in Chapter 2.

Following the early team-building activities, there are other specific areas which call for the attention of team members in order to further team development. This section of the manual provides directions for:
1. increasing team members' skill in listening
2. building on other members' contributions
3. asking helpful questions
4. improving members' skills in participating effectively in group discussions
5. effectively using individual members' skills in the working of the team.

An Activity to Aid in Listening with Understanding
(60 minutes in groups of seven or eight persons)

Purpose: To increase team-member skill in listening carefully in order to understand what the speaker *intends* to say.

Step 1 — 15 minutes. Ask one member to express his opinion about a question of interest to the whole group, such as "What are your feelings about children watching television?" The person next to him then repeats back the meaning of what the first member said to the satisfaction of the first member. The second member then states

16

his opinion. Then the member next to him repeats back what the second member said, and gives his own opinion, and so on around the circle until everyone has practiced repeating back.

Step 2 — 15 minutes. Using a more personal question, such as "What are some of your problems in communicating with others?" repeat the procedure in Step 1.

Step 3 — 15 minutes. Using the question, "How do you feel about the last thirty minutes?" repeat the procedure in Step 1 with one exception. Instead of going around the circle, have the person who speaks point to the person he wants to repeat back the meaning of what he has just said and in turn to be the next speaker.

Step 4 — 15 minutes. In the total group respond to the question: "What did you learn about listening?" Team members speak spontaneously in brief phrases or one sentence only. Members *do not* react to each other's responses. This procedure permits sharing of personal learnings by brainstorming.

AN ACTIVITY TO BUILD ON MEMBER CONTRIBUTIONS (30 minutes)

Purpose: To increase team-member skill in responding directly to the contributions of other members.

Step 1 — 25 minutes. During a regular team meeting while the group is working on any task, practice the following: to each verbal contribution made by any member of the team a direct verbal response must be made from the next speaker. The response may be of any kind, a question or a suggestion, but it must be directly in response to what the person speaking has just said. For example, if the planning committee for a women's group is trying to decide what topics will be covered in monthly meetings next year, Mary Jones may say, "Why don't we have a speaker on student movements on college campuses?" Paula answers, "Please say more of what you have in mind, Mary." Mary's reply may be, "A lot of us have children in high school and college, and I'd like to know more about what is happening." Joan responds, "That is a real concern, Mary, and reminds me that one of the mothers of some preschool children in our group was telling me she'd like to have someone talk about religious training in the home." Each speaker builds on the contribution of the previous one so that individual verbal contributions enlarge understanding and give new insights into the problem. These may be illustrated as links in a chain.

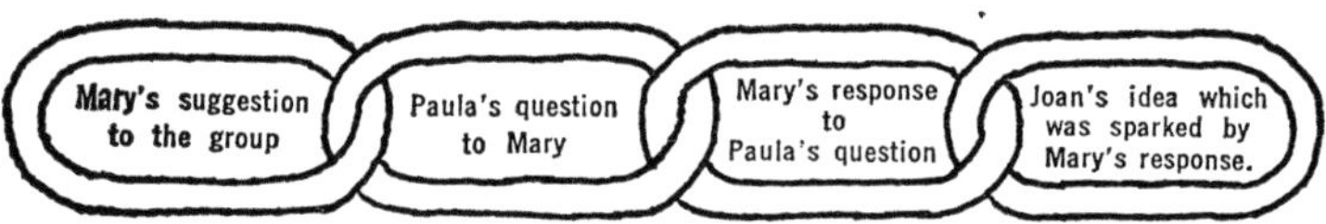

Step 2 — 5 minutes. As a total team discuss: "What have we learned about the way we respond to each other's verbal contributions?"

AN ACTIVITY TO AID IN
ASKING HELPFUL QUESTIONS (45 minutes)

Purpose: To increase skill in asking questions that encourage dialogue in the group.

Step 1 — Divide into groups of three (persons *a, b, c*) for 30 minutes. Allow each person 10 minutes to ask questions concerning the barriers which prevent the team from achieving its objectives. For 3–4 minutes *a* asks *b* questions; *c* writes down which questions were helpful, which were not helpful. For 6–7 minutes *b* and *c* tell *a* which questions were helpful and which were not helpful and give their reasons.

18

For 10 minutes — Repeat with *b* asking *c* questions; *a* taking notes.

For 10 minutes — Repeat with *c* asking *a* questions; *b* taking notes.

Step 2 — Allow 10 minutes to distribute and discuss copies of "A Guide to Asking Questions" below. (This should be mimeographed for use in the session.)

Step 3 — Then discuss: "What have I learned about asking questions?" If the team has more than twelve members, discuss in two groups.

A GUIDE TO ASKING QUESTIONS

Do:

Ask questions that call for more than "yes" or "no" answers.

Ask questions so that others are encouraged to respond with their ideas. (*What* do you think about that idea?)

Ask in a way which makes clear that you don't think you have the answer.

Relate questions to the purpose of the meeting. (Stick to the point.)

Ask questions about feelings as well as information. (How do you *feel* about that?)

Focus questions on one point. (Who, what, when, how?)

Ask for concrete facts of what was said and done, when, by whom, where.

Don't:

Ask questions that can be answered "yes" or "no."

Ask threatening or motivational questions. (*Why* do you think that?)

Try to lead others to your answer.

Lead the team to an unrelated topic.

Ask purely theoretical questions. (What is the meaning of . . . ?)

Ask rhetorical questions. (Don't you think that . . . ?)

Ask what *should* have been done. (No one knows!)

An Activity to Build More
Effective Team Membership (90 minutes)

Purpose: To increase team members' skills in participating helpfully in team discussions.

Step 1 — 10 minutes. Arbitrarily divide the team in half. Ask one half to form an inner circle and to participate in a 10-minute discussion of a topic, such as (a) how they feel about what the team is doing, (b) how satisfactory is being a member of this team, or (c) some of the problems they see the team having. Ask the other half of the group to form an outer circle and to observe intently and silently what happens during the discussion, noting on paper *specific* things persons say and do that (1) are helpful in moving the discussion along or (2) block the movement of the discussion. (An alternative is to assign each observer to watch one particular participant during the discussion.)

Step 2 — 20 minutes. Observers, taking turns, quickly share what they noted participants specifically say or do that was helpful or hindering. Participants add any additional observations. Caution: observers should try to be objective, not judgmental; participants should try to be open, not defensive. Everyone needs to avoid continuing to discuss the topic of the first 10 minutes. Discuss *what happened* and its *effect* on the discussion in Step 1. Break for 5 minutes before Step 3.

Step 3 — 10 minutes, and Step 4 — 20 minutes. Repeat steps 1 and 2, alternating participants and observers in the inner and outer circles. The participants may discuss the same topic as stated in Step 1 or a different topic may be assigned to them.

Step 5 — 10 minutes. The total team together now lists on newsprint the helpful things that members can do for the sake of the team and its work.

20

Step 6 — 10–20 minutes. Hand out copies of the following list of helpful member functions to supplement those already listed by the team on newsprint.

To help the team to fulfill its task, members need to: (In each case, the suggestions are given as examples, not as an exhaustive list, of what may be done.)

1. *Initiate:* Propose tasks; define a problem; suggest a procedure or ideas for solving a problem.
2. *Seek information or opinions:* Request facts; seek relevant information; ask for expressions of feeling; seek suggestions and ideas.
3. *Give information or opinions:* Offer facts; provide relevant information; state a belief about a matter before the team; give suggestions and ideas.
4. *Clarify and elaborate:* Interpret ideas or suggestions; clear up confusions; define terms; indicate alternatives and issues before the team.
5. *Summarize:* Pull together related ideas; summarize suggestions after the group has discussed them; offer a decision or conclusion for the group to accept or reject.
6. *Test consensus:* Ask if the group is nearing a decision; send up a "trial balloon" to test a possible conclusion by saying something like, "Are we ready to agree that we take the following steps?"

To help the team to have good relationships which provide for maximum use of individual resources, members need to:

1. *Harmonize:* Attempt to reconcile disagreements; reduce tensions; get people to explore differences.
2. *Gate keep:* Help to keep communication channels open; facilitate the participation of others; suggest procedures that permit sharing remarks.
3. *Encourage:* Be friendly and responsive to others; indicate by expressions or remarks the acceptance of others' contributions.
4. *Compromise:* When your own idea or status is in-

volved in a conflict, offer a compromise which yields status; admit error; modify your position in interest of group cohesion or growth.

5. *Set and test standards:* Test whether group is satisfied with its procedures or wants to suggest new procedures.

An Activity to Strengthen Team Relationships
(Time needed will vary according to the size of the team. A team of eight probably will need 90 minutes.)

Purpose: To provide a specific way for team members to receive from each other helpful suggestions for increasing their effectiveness on the team.

Explain to the entire team the purpose and procedure of the activity. Allow time for individuals to volunteer to receive responses from their teammates. There needs to be as little pressure as possible.

One by one, each member who is willing asks others who are willing to: (1) tell him what they see are his strengths as a member of the team and (2) suggest how they would like to see him use his gifts and skills more effectively for the team in the future. Repeat the experience for everyone who wants a turn.

For example: Charlie volunteers. He says, "I'd be happy to have anybody who wants to tell me what he sees are my strengths as a member of this team." Harry answers, "Charlie, what you just did in being first to ask for our reactions illustrates to me one of your strengths: always willing to participate fully and try out whatever is suggested." May adds, "I agree with Harry, Charlie, and you are very warm and open in your participation." After several other comments Charlie says, "Thanks, team, now tell me, how would you like to see me change so I'd be more helpful." "OK," says Blanche. "At times you seem to me to push us toward a decision when I sense we aren't through discussing the problem. For example, a little while ago you said, 'We're all agreed on this training program for teachers — let's move on.' I felt there were other factors to be considered, but your positive tone and emphasis caused me to be hesitant to speak up and say so." After several other suggestions to Charlie, he again says thanks. Then Tom speaks up to be next. The group continues discussing both the person's strengths and the suggestions for his improved participation until each person who wants a turn has had it.

AN ACTIVITY TO AID TEAMS IN MAKING
DECISIONS EFFECTIVELY (For the entire meeting period)

Purpose: To help the team to gain skill and satisfaction in making decisions.

Post on newsprint the following questions:
1. *What* are we trying to decide? (Be sure this is clear to everyone.)
2. What *alternatives* do we have? (Consider as many as possible.)
3. How may each alternative *work?*
4. *Which* alternative or *combination* of alternatives do we choose?
5. What do we need to *do to carry out* the decision?
6. *Who* will do *what, when?* (Be specific.)

Whenever during the meeting the team is faced with a decision, focus on these questions and answer them in order. Before the session is completed, the group should evaluate its effectiveness in making decisions.

A PERIODIC CHECKUP ON "TEAM HEALTH"
AND ACHIEVEMENT OF OBJECTIVES

Purpose: To provide an opportunity for team members to examine how they feel about each other in relation to satisfaction with the team or its achievement of objectives.

A. Satisfaction with the Team (50 minutes)

Step 1 — 10 minutes. Each member lists the name of every person in the circle including himself, and writes a number between 0 and 20 by his name and the name of each other person. Numbers indicate how satisfied he feels each person is with the team. (20 would indicate complete satisfaction, 0 no satisfaction). Each person should be encouraged to record honestly how he feels.

Step 2 — 10 minutes. Post newsprint with the names of each person, two or three to each sheet. Each person writes his own number *next* to his name and the number he has assigned to each other person *under* that person's name on the newsprint.

Step 3 — 30 minutes. Each member may ask the reasons a number was given him if he wishes to learn why it was given.

B. Satisfaction with Team Achievement of Objectives (50 minutes)

Steps 1 and 2 — 20 minutes. Have team objectives posted on newsprint. Use Steps 1 and 2 listed for the previous activity, "Satisfaction with the Team." Here numbers indicate how satisfied the recorder feels each person is with the achievement of team objectives.

Step 3 — 15 minutes. Each member may ask the reasons for any low numbers given by others. Each member who gave himself a low number may share his reasons.

Step 4 — 15 minutes. The total team should discuss: "What changes can be made in what we are doing as a team to increase our satisfaction with our achievement of objectives?"

4.
Brief Evaluation of Team Meetings

In continuing to strengthen the team's ability to work purposively together it is profitable to spend time in evaluation at the end of each meeting. The purpose of such evaluation is to allow for direct personal expression of feelings before ending the meeting and to get ideas for specific ways to improve future team meetings. Make sure each person has an opportunity to say what he feels. Choose a different procedure for doing this in various meetings. Six suggestions follow:

IDENTIFYING FEELINGS (20 minutes)

Step 1—2 or 3 minutes. On newsprint one person writes: "What one word describes your feelings about this meeting?" Allow for silent reflection. Each person writes his word on a small card or piece of paper, and turns the paper face down before him.

Step 2 — 10 to 12 minutes. One at a time each person shows the others what he wrote and says what happened in the meeting which caused him to write what he did. For example, Harry turns up his card and says, "I wrote *relieved*. I feel relieved because we have made so many decisions about the Christmas program that I think it will work well this year." Martha says, "I wrote *disappointed* because I missed the suggestions of the four members who weren't able to be here."

Step 3 — 5 minutes. The total team discusses the question: "Based on what has been said, in what specific ways will we try to do things differently at our next meeting?"

Identifying Strengths and Weaknesses (16 minutes)

Step 1 — 5 to 6 minutes. On newsprint a volunteer writes: "I feel the strengths of our meeting were. . . ." Allow two or three minutes for silent reflection. Team members then respond verbally, spontaneously in brief phrases or in one sentence. Mike may say, "I liked the fact that we were all here and that we started on time." Loretta may say, "I liked the fact that the committee for the youth camp brought in a proposal on newsprint. That gave us a starting point for our discussion."

Step 2 — 2 to 5 minutes. One writes on newsprint: "I feel the weaknesses of our meeting were. . . ." Allow a minute for silent reflection. Repeat the procedure of having team members respond verbally and spontaneously. Grace may say, "I wish we met more often. I feel that we were slow getting the discussion flowing because we had forgotten so much about the matters that we discussed last month."

Step 3 — 5 minutes. The total team discusses the question: "Based on what has been said, in what specific ways will we try to do things differently at our next meeting?"

Evaluating Verbal Participation (11 minutes)

Step 1 — For 15 minutes preceding the evaluation period have one member record the verbal participation of all team members. (See illustration below.) The person drawing up the chart makes a circle of the names of those present on a blank 8½x11 sheet. He writes the names in the order in which persons are seated in the circle. Each time a person speaks, he places a small vertical line (1) beside his name and draws an arrow indicating to whom he spoke. For example, if Bob spoke to Bill a 1 would go beside Bill's name and an arrow would be drawn from Bill's name to Bob's on the chart. If Bill made his remark to the whole group, the arrow would go from Bill's name to the middle of the circle.

Step 2 — 2 to 3 minutes. The person who has made the participation chart reports to the group. He shows them the chart and says, "As you can see Bob spoke eight times; Dot spoke five times; Dick four times; Thelma, Joe, and Bill each once; and Harold and Mary did not speak during this 15-minute period."

Step 3 — 7 to 8 minutes. The whole team responds verbally, spontaneously to this report. Bob may say, "I was conscious of talking a lot. Does anyone feel I was dominating the conversation?" Dick may add, "Bob, you and Dot and I sure had more to say than anybody else. I'd say if there was any take-over of the discussion it was by the three of us as a subgroup." Joe may agree, "Yes, Dick, I think you have a good point. The three of you keep the verbal ball bouncing between you. After my one suggestion wasn't picked up, I just decided to listen." Mary adds, "I felt I didn't know much about what we were discussing, so I thought I'd keep quiet too, but I felt a little uncomfortable remaining silent." The conversation continues until everyone who wants to say how he felt about his or another's participation has spoken.

Step 4 — 5 minutes. The total team discusses the question: "In what specific ways can we improve our verbal participation in team discussion?" Bob may say, "Next time I feel like I'm talking too much, I think I'll say that I'm feeling that way and ask, 'What do some of the rest of you think?' " Joe may say, "The next time I feel cut out, I'm going to say so and see what happens." Mary might volunteer, "Before our next meeting, I'll try to find out more about the subject."

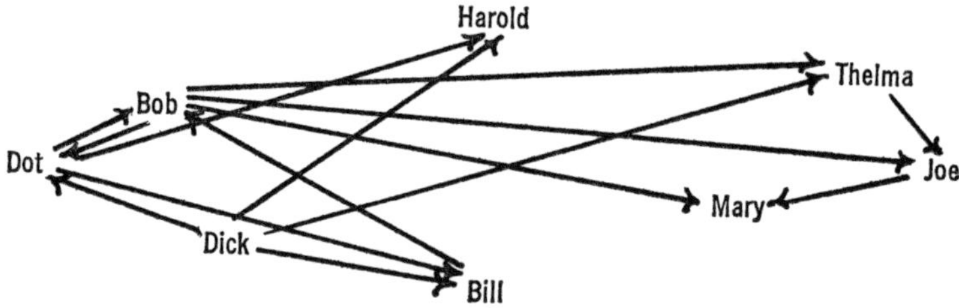

ANALYZING FEELINGS (15 minutes)

Step 1 — 5 minutes. Post several sheets of newsprint in a line. Across the top a volunteer writes, "The way I feel about this meeting is. . . ." Have each member use felt tip pens to write a word or phrase or make a drawing to give his response to the open-ended sentence. See illustration:

Step 2 — 5 minutes. One at a time team members say what they meant. For example, in the illustration above, Phil explains, "I drew hearts and flowers because I felt we were being too polite and not saying how we really felt." Joan adds, "Maybe what I felt about not enough participation fits in with that, Phil." Susan says, "I wrote 'A good meeting but slow,' and that ties in with the lack of everyone speaking." "All those question marks around my head," says Paula, "are there because, as I think about the meeting, I'm not sure what was happening." "That's what my 'HELP' meant," agrees Pete. "I'm confused, too." "You all can see my sunrise, can't you?" asks Carl. "I feel there is hope, but the light is just beginning to dawn."

28

Step 3 — 5 minutes. The total group quickly lists responses to the following question without discussing the responses: "What specifically will we try to do differently at our next meeting?" Using the illustration above, some responses may be: "Be more frank in stating opinions." "Ask silent members what they think." "Say when I'm confused."

USING SIMILES TO EXPRESS FEELINGS (17 minutes)

Step 1 — 3 to 4 minutes. Everyone closes his eyes and silently imagines a situation where he and the rest of the team *might be*. One person may imagine the team on a moving bus; another may think of the team on a picnic in a park; another may envision the team playing a softball game. Whatever pops into one's head, he goes on silently to imagine the continuing action of the picture in his mind.

Step 2 — 7 to 8 minutes. One by one persons share briefly and verbally what they imagined and how they see it relating to their feelings about the meeting. For example: Jack imagined the group on the bus. He says: "Right away I wanted to see who was the driver, and it was you, Dick. You looked happy and relaxed at the wheel, as I feel you were in being chairman of the meeting tonight. The bus was going through lovely countryside — not too fast — and I feel this meeting has been that kind of a pleasant trip. The thing that bothers me is that I feel the rest of us were along for the ride tonight. When Dick presented ideas, we didn't react much."

Step 3 — 5 minutes. The total team quickly responds, without discussing responses to: "What will we try to do differently in our next meeting?" Using the illustration above, Jack may say, "I'd *respond* more to the chairman's suggestions and encourage others to do the same."

Step 1 — 2 or 3 minutes. One person asks each member to think quickly of a food or color that comes to mind when he thinks of the meeting the team has just had. He allows time for each person to record his word on a small card or piece of paper.

Step 2 — 10 minutes. One at a time each person shares his word and its implication as a description of the meeting. For example, Jane says, "Pink — the meeting was kind of sweet and soft. I was being

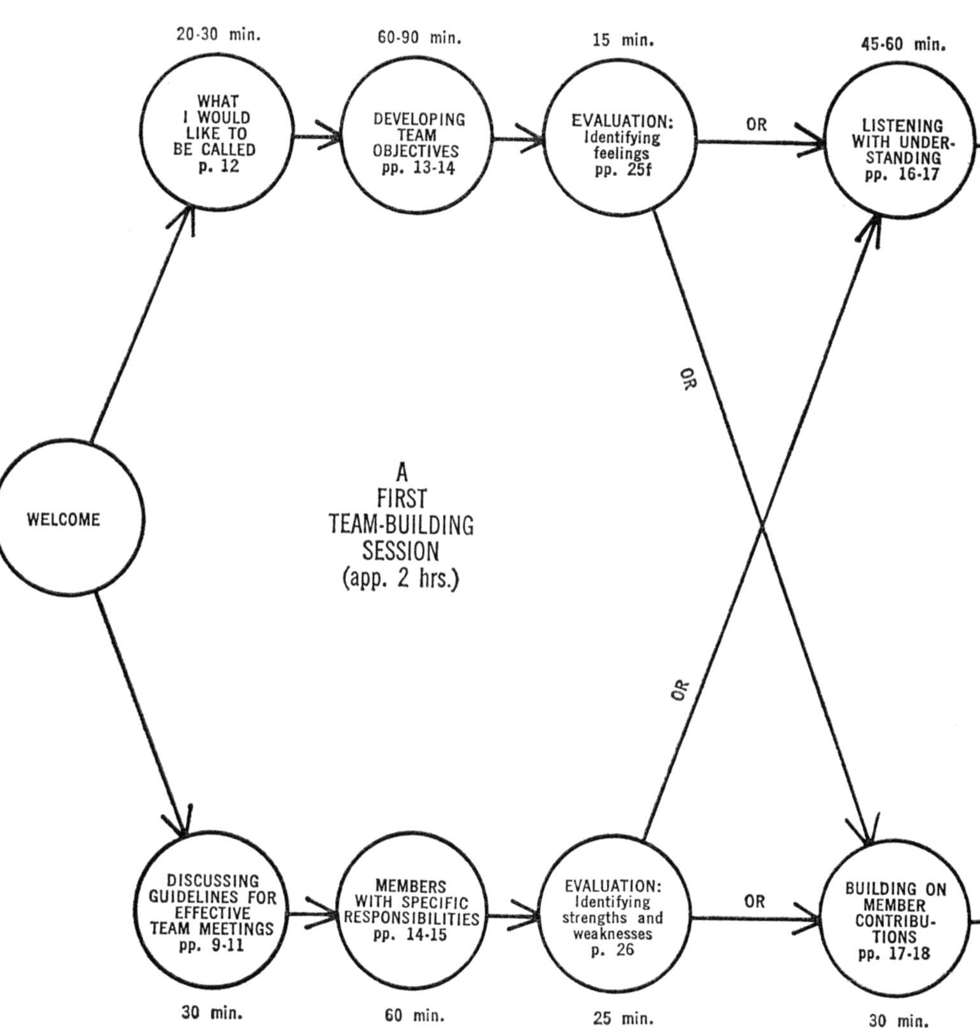

nice and polite." "Like cotton candy, that's my food," adds Paul. "Sticky, sweet." Carl echoes, "Squash. We had squash for dinner—bland, mild, no bite, nothing I could get my teeth into."

Step 3 — 5 minutes. The total team discusses the question:"Based on what has been said, what will we try to do differently in our next meeting?" From the illustration above, some reactions may be: "Stop being polite and also voice disagreements or dissatisfactions." "Challenge the climate of the group." "Ask what is going on."

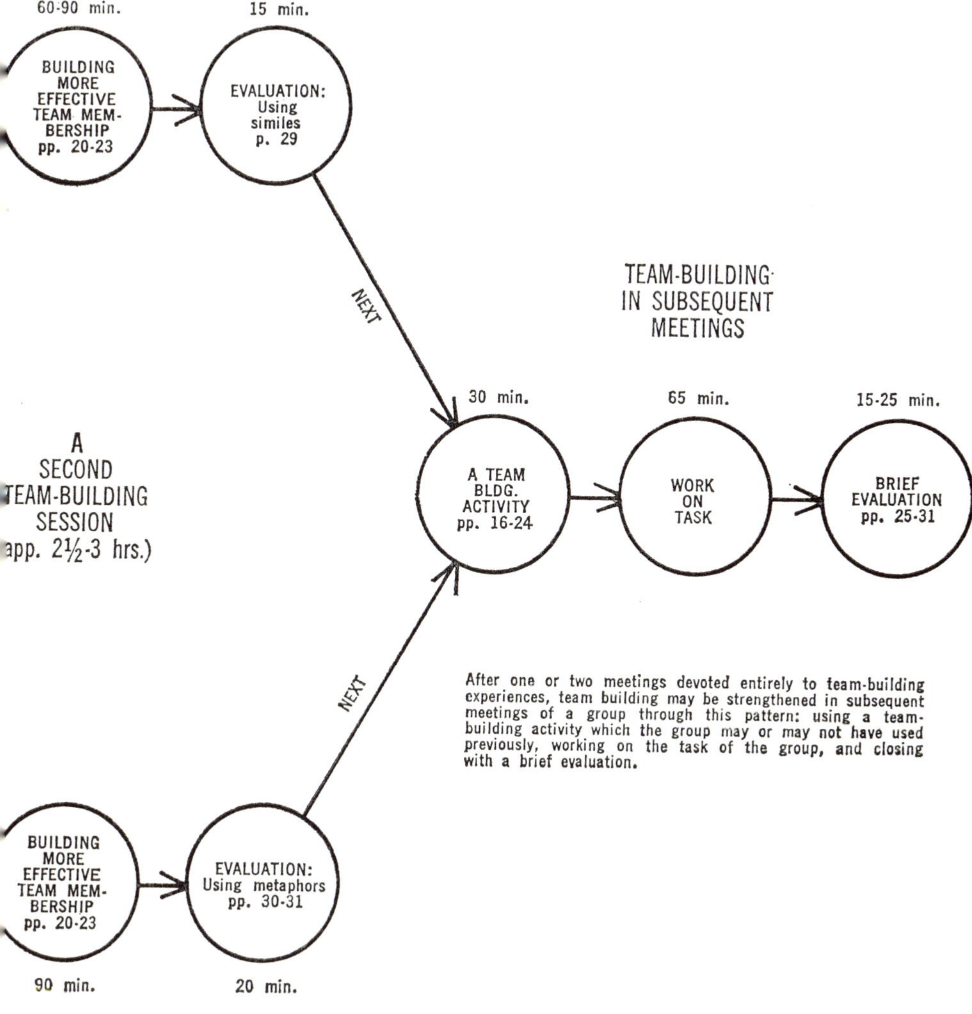

5.
Never Completed

Team building is an ongoing process for every group of people who work together on a common task. Whether or not team building occurs is dependent on the willingness of the team members to believe in and act on the goals of team building. When team members openly express their feelings, ideas, and concerns related to the task, and when they listen and respond directly to other team members, team building takes place. When team members act on the Apostle Paul's statement that Christians are "one body" in which each member is indispensable, equally concerned, and responsible for every other member, team building occurs. Basically, this experience of being members of one body in Christ comes not from following procedures or activities but through the interaction of team members who believe in and act on the goals of team building.

No team ever *arrives;* team building is *never completed.* To think so leads to complacency, insensitivity, and stagnation. Team building is an exciting and dynamic process in which members continuously engage as they come together to work on a common task. The challenge and call to new life inherent in team building is always open to those who will respond.